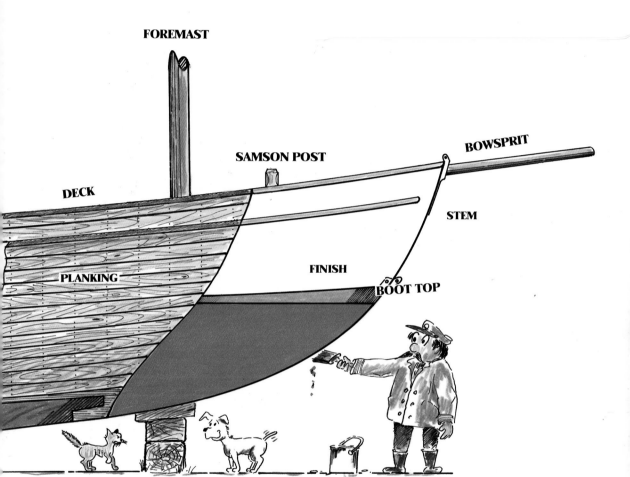

FOREMAST

SAMSON POST

BOWSPRIT

DECK

STEM

PLANKING

FINISH

BOOT TOP

PLANKING

FINISH

BOATING

with Cap'n Bob
and Matey

AN ENCYCLOPEDIA FOR KIDS OF ALL AGES

Illustrations by BOBBY BASNIGHT
Text by LEW HACKLER

SEASCAPE ENTERPRISES

Colonial Heights, VA, U.S.A.

NOTE: The glossary at the back contains many of the everyday words used around boats by those who are interested in boating. These words are intentionally given a very simple definition to make them easy to remember.

SEASCAPE ENTERPRISES
P.O. Box 176
Colonial Heights, VA 23834

For Stacy, Brian, Cassie, and Cade
and for my Second Mate, Matey.

Grateful acknowledgment is made to Charles E. Kanter, Sea Captain, boat surveyor, boating consultant, and writer, for checking the Glossary; to Jonathan Eaton, Editor, International Marine Publishing, Mariellen Eaton, and Matthew Eaton, each of whom made a number of valuable suggestions; and to Patricia Rychlik Blaszak for her good advice and editing.

A

"Fetch the paddle, Matey," yells Cap'n Bob. "It's ADRIFT."

Let's take a trip with Cap'n Bob and Matey to see the BOATS and have some fun. There is a lot to learn and a lot to do. It's more fun when you know what to call things.

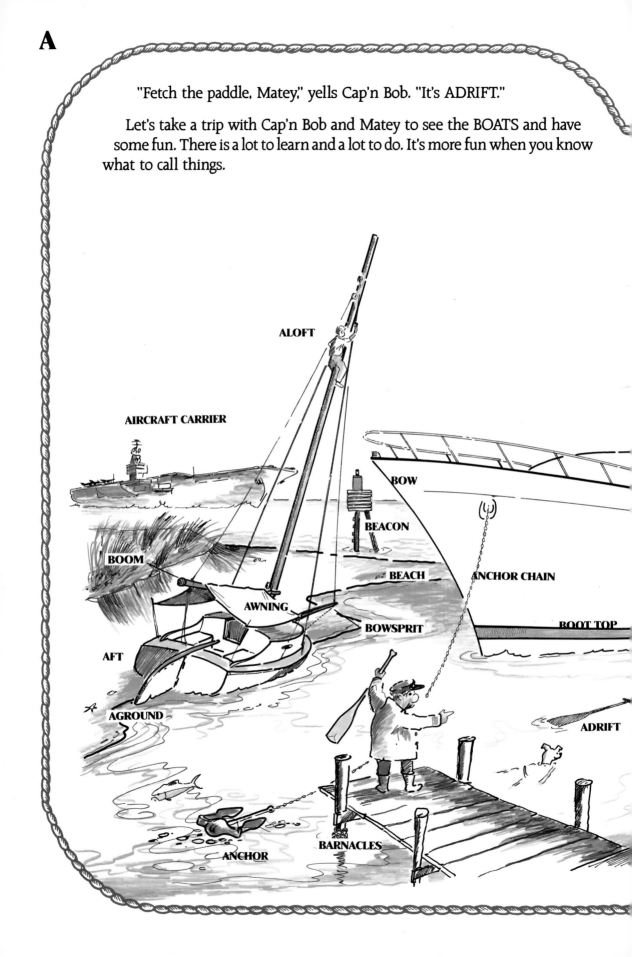

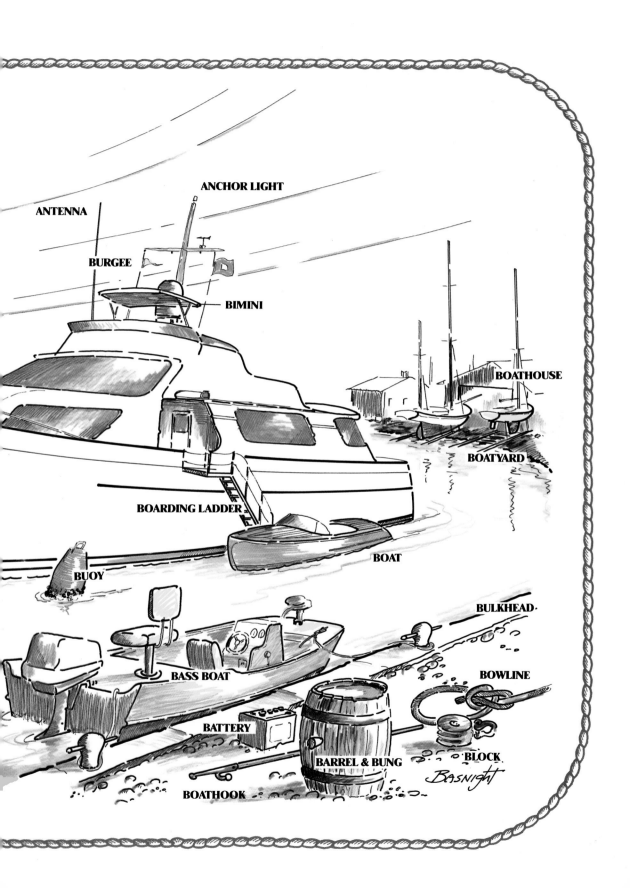

ANCHOR LIGHT

ANTENNA

BURGEE

BIMINI

BOATHOUSE

BOATYARD

BOARDING LADDER

BOAT

BUOY

BULKHEAD

BOWLINE

BASS BOAT

BATTERY

BARREL & BUNG

BLOCK

BOATHOOK

BASNIGHT

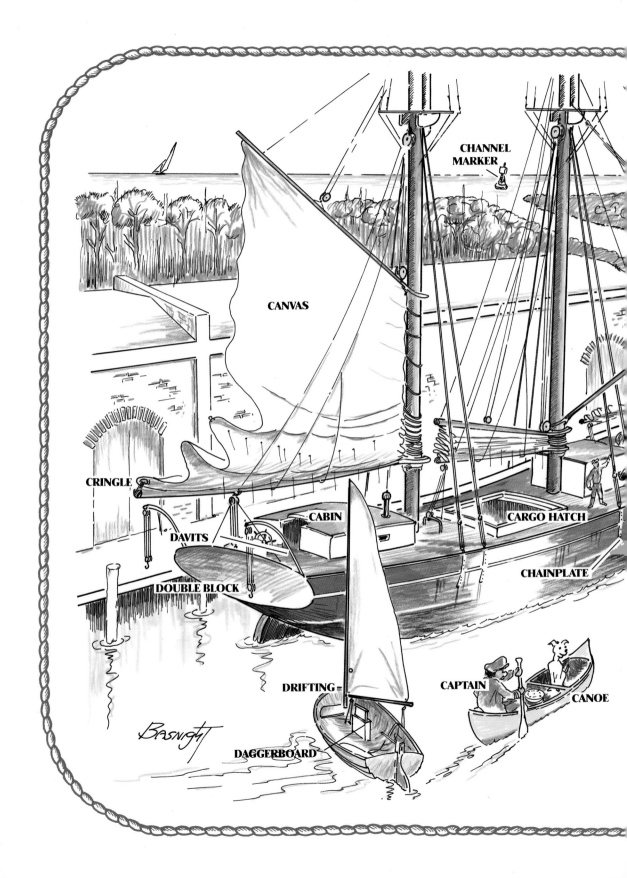

CHANNEL MARKER

CANVAS

CRINGLE

CABIN

CARGO HATCH

DAVITS

CHAINPLATE

DOUBLE BLOCK

DRIFTING

CAPTAIN

CANOE

BASNIGHT

DAGGERBOARD

Cap'n Bob paddles the CANOE to head off the DRIFTING sailboat. But Matey sees a DIVER and barks to Cap'n Bob to stay clear. Lots of things can happen around boats, and boats are always moving around. Sometimes they move when you least expect it.

Matey knows he has to be very careful around boats.

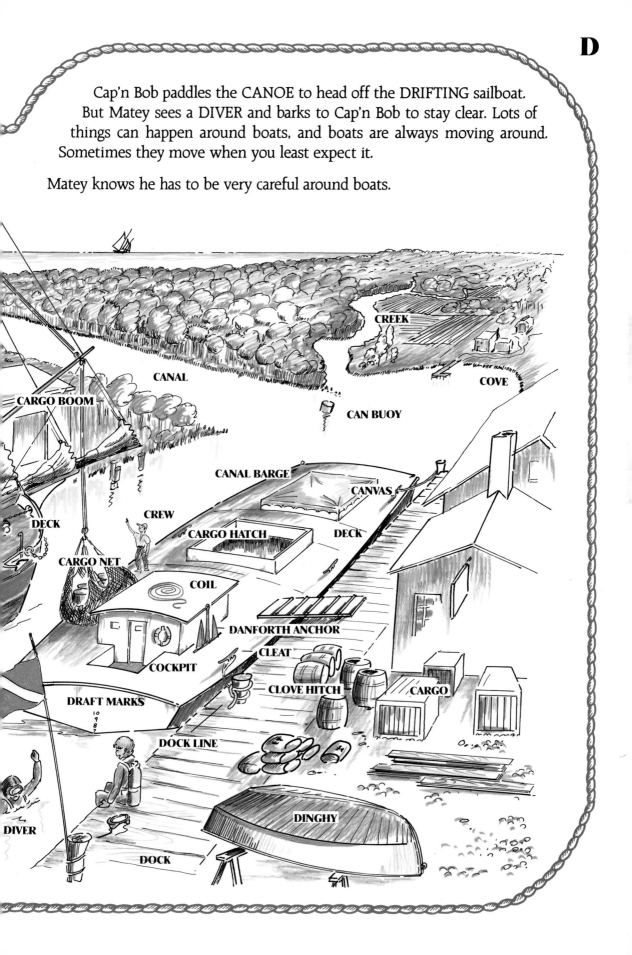

CREEK

CANAL

COVE

CARGO BOOM

CAN BUOY

CANAL BARGE

CANVAS

CREW

DECK

CARGO HATCH

DECK

CARGO NET

COIL

DANFORTH ANCHOR

CLEAT

COCKPIT

CLOVE HITCH

CARGO

DRAFT MARKS

DOCK LINE

DIVER

DINGHY

DOCK

Matey was going to bark, but Sue turned out of the way just in time. Sue sees a FLARE in the sky, and a GUST of wind coming. She'll be ready when the wind hits her sails. Sue knows she has to keep a sharp lookout and always to hold on.

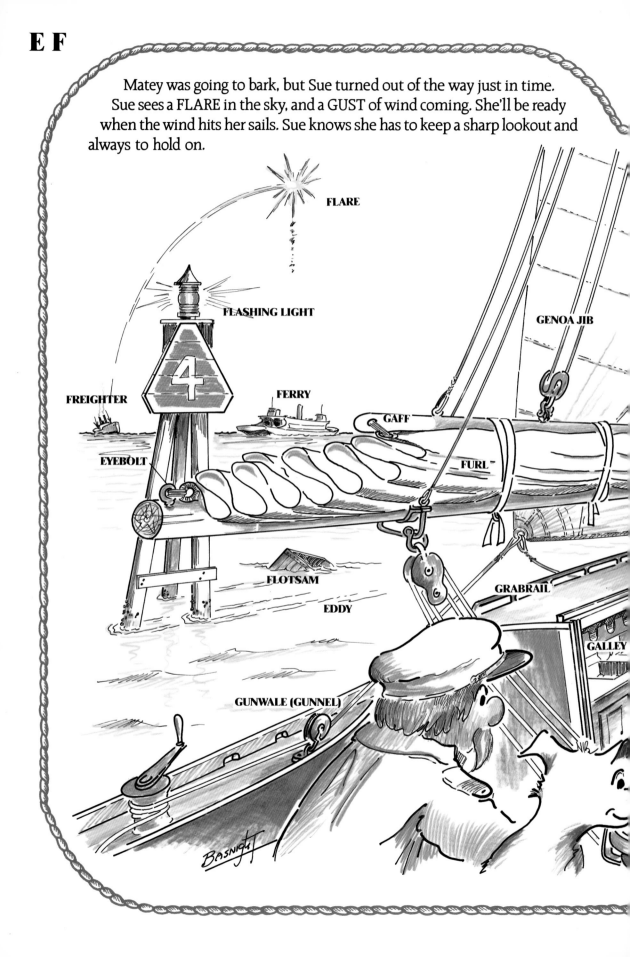

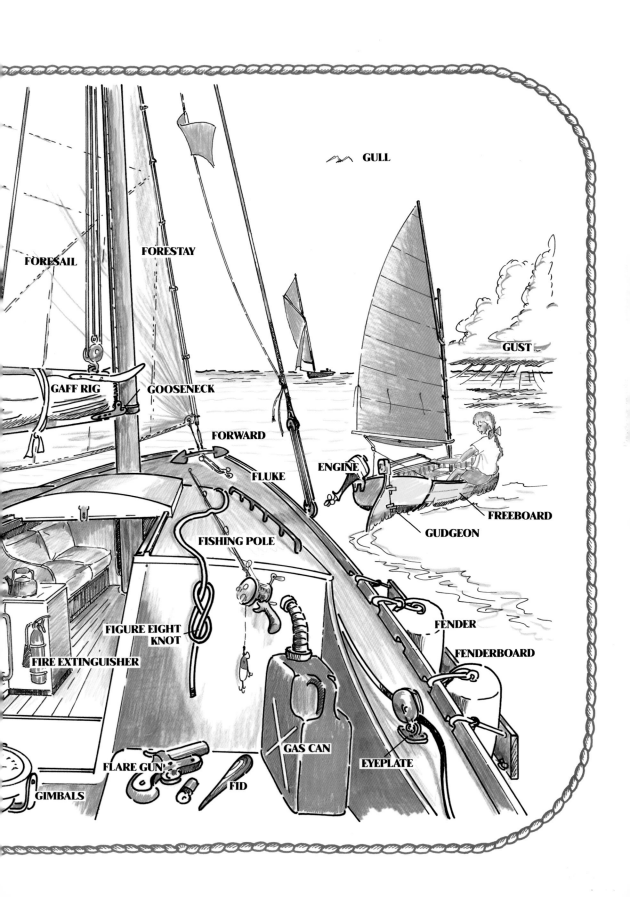

GULL

FORESTAY

FORESAIL

GUST

GAFF RIG

GOOSENECK

FORWARD

ENGINE

FLUKE

FREEBOARD

GUDGEON

FISHING POLE

FENDER

FIGURE EIGHT
KNOT

FENDERBOARD

FIRE EXTINGUISHER

GAS CAN

FLARE GUN

EYEPLATE

FID

GIMBALS

Cap'n Bob always wears rubber soled shoes when he goes aboard a boat. He and Matey know that they must always be careful not to slip or trip on decks and docks.

Cap'n Bob and Matey want to go sailing, but first they must repair the HULL and the HALYARD.

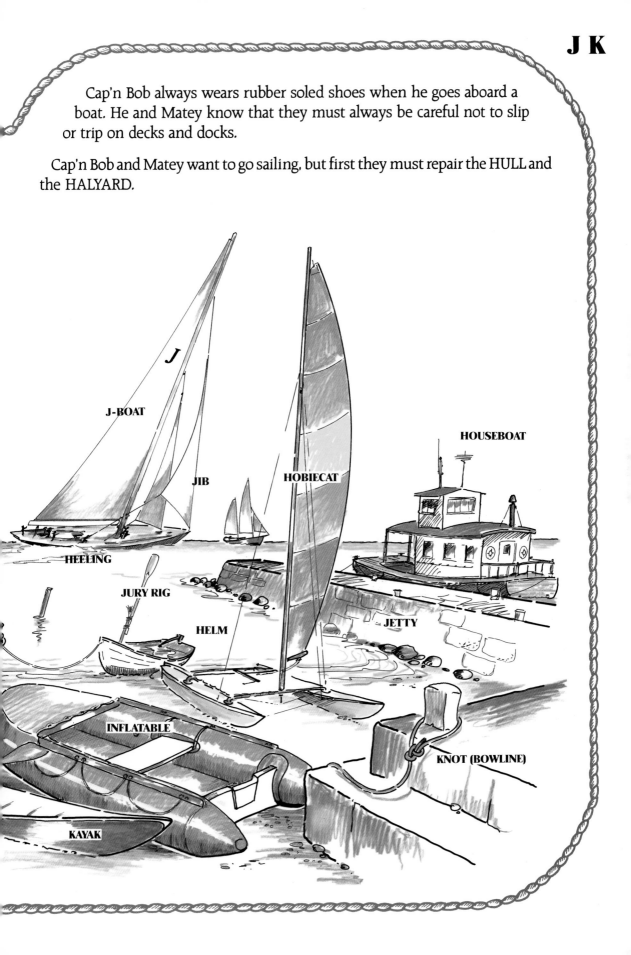

L

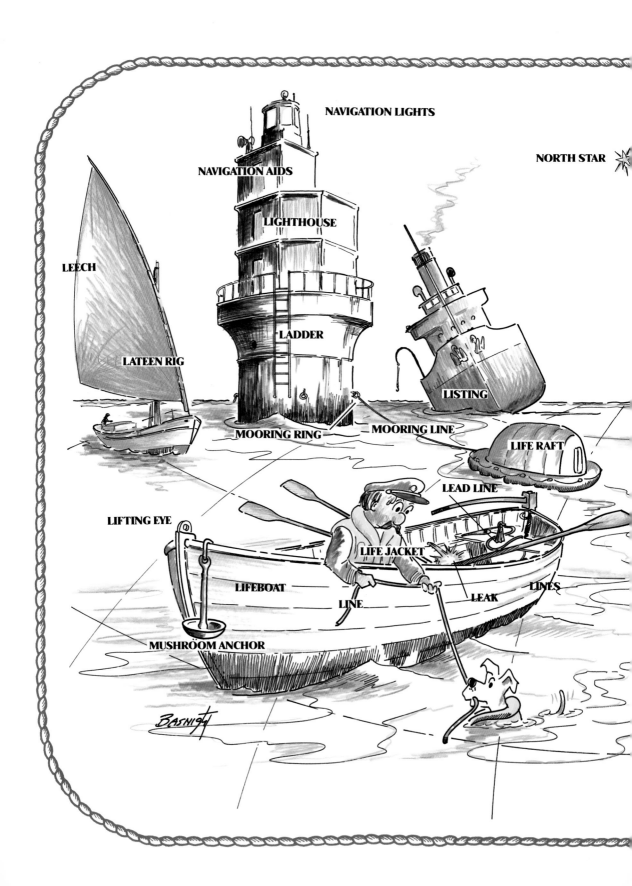

NAVIGATION LIGHTS

NORTH STAR

NAVIGATION AIDS

LEECH

LIGHTHOUSE

LATEEN RIG

LADDER

LISTING

MOORING RING

MOORING LINE

LIFE RAFT

LEAD LINE

LIFTING EYE

LIFE JACKET

LIFEBOAT

LINE

LEAK

LINES

MUSHROOM ANCHOR

BASNIGHT

Matey knows the Captain is always in charge even in a small LIFEBOAT. When you go on a boat, find out where the LIFE JACKETS are kept and how to put one on. Don't be afraid to ask the Captain about anything you want to know.

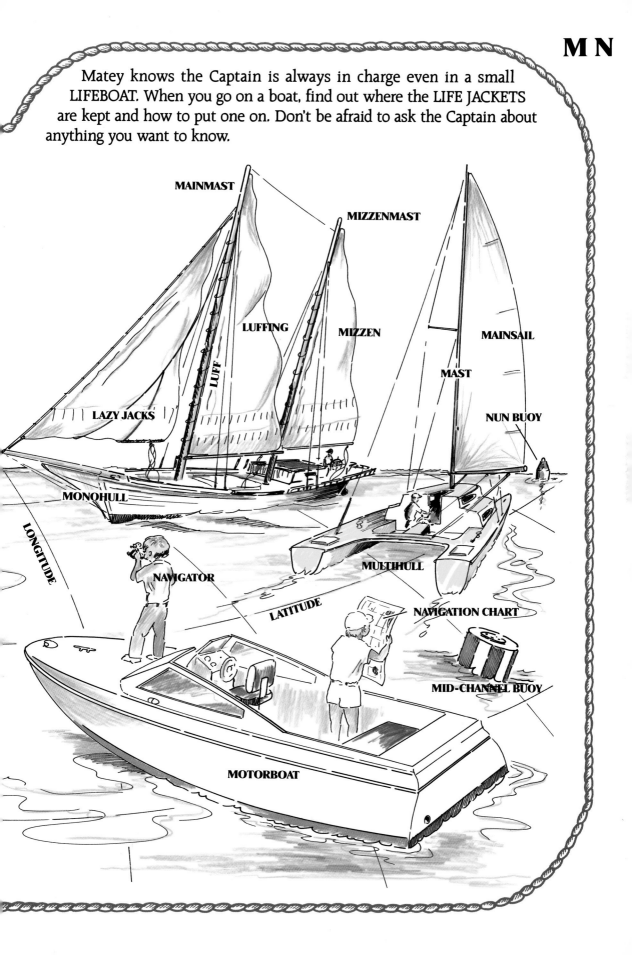

MAINMAST

MIZZENMAST

LUFFING

MIZZEN

MAINSAIL

MAST

LUFF

NUN BUOY

LAZY JACKS

MONOHULL

LONGITUDE

NAVIGATOR

MULTIHULL

LATITUDE

NAVIGATION CHART

MID-CHANNEL BUOY

MOTORBOAT

o

Matey's ready to help, but they see some QUICK ACTION on the PIER. Later, when they go back to the boat, each item they bought while in PORT will be stowed (stored) in a certain place, so it will be easy to find when it's needed.

PENNANT

PULLEY

OIL LAMP

OARLOCKS

ONE DESIGN

PULPIT

"OLD SALT"

OUTBOARD MOTOR

PORT (SIDE)

PADEYE

PINTAL

PALM

PLIERS

PARALLEL RUL

PAINT

PROPELLER

PLOW ANCHOR

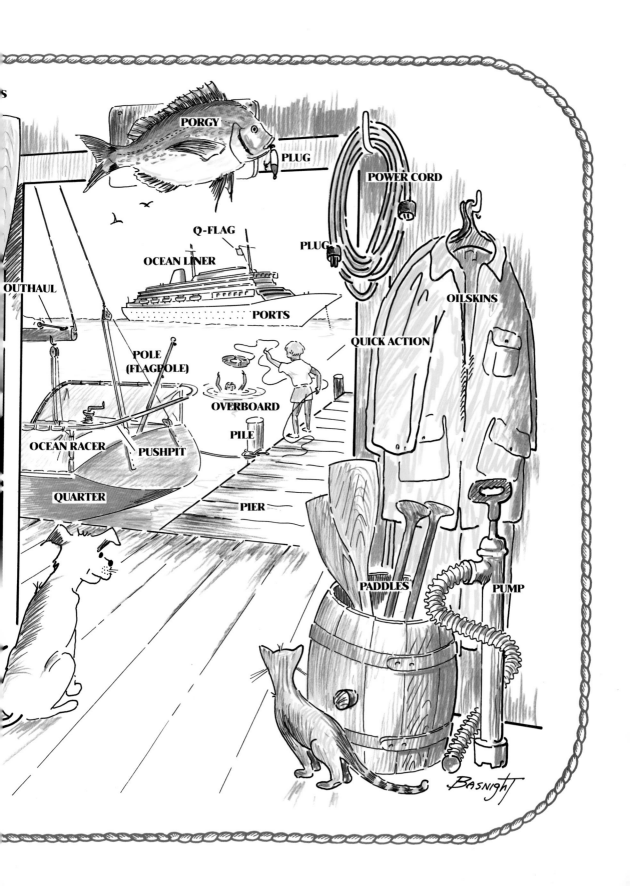

RAFTING UP is lots of fun, and a good chance for Cap'n Bob and Matey to make new friends. Sometimes the boats are tied STEM to STERN. It's also a good time to learn new things. Ask the SKIPPER to help you learn how to tie a SQUARE KNOT.

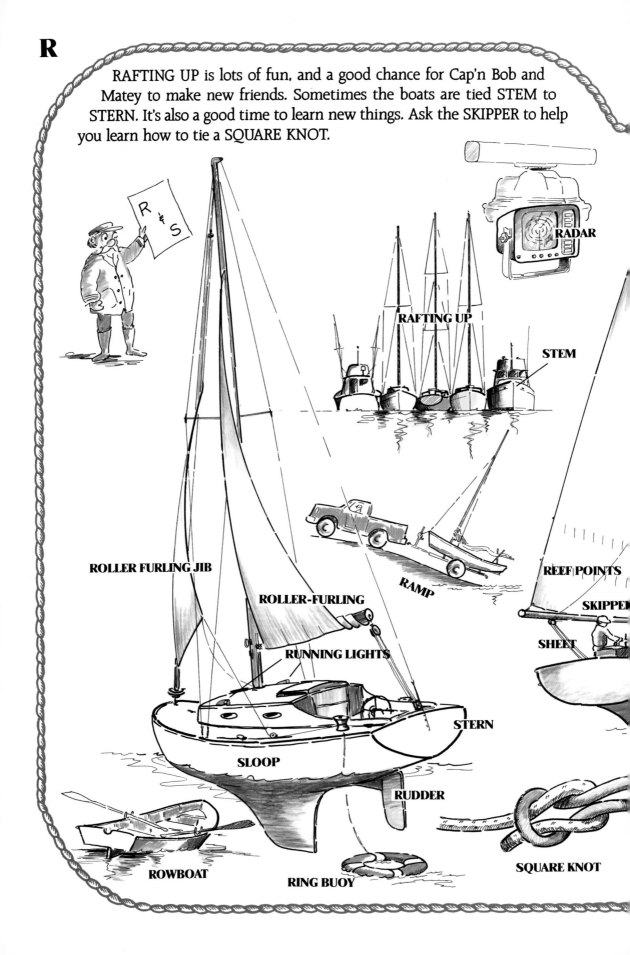

RADAR

RAFTING UP

STEM

ROLLER FURLING JIB

ROLLER-FURLING

REEF POINTS

SKIPPER

RAMP

SHEET

RUNNING LIGHTS

STERN

SLOOP

RUDDER

ROWBOAT

RING BUOY

SQUARE KNOT

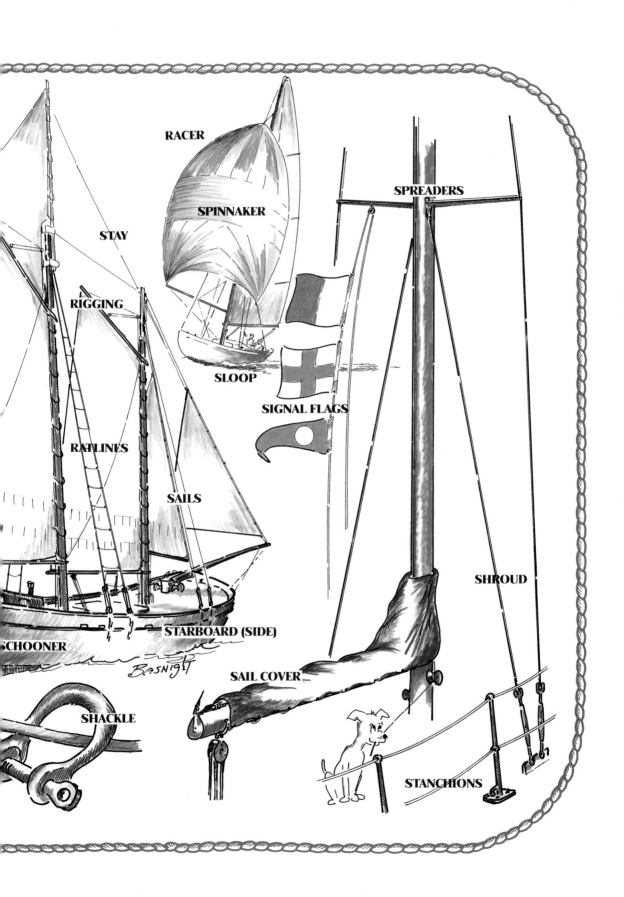

RACER

STAY

RIGGING

SPINNAKER

SLOOP

SPREADERS

SIGNAL FLAGS

RATLINES

SAILS

SHROUD

STARBOARD (SIDE)

SCHOONER

Basnight

SAIL COVER

SHACKLE

STANCHIONS

T

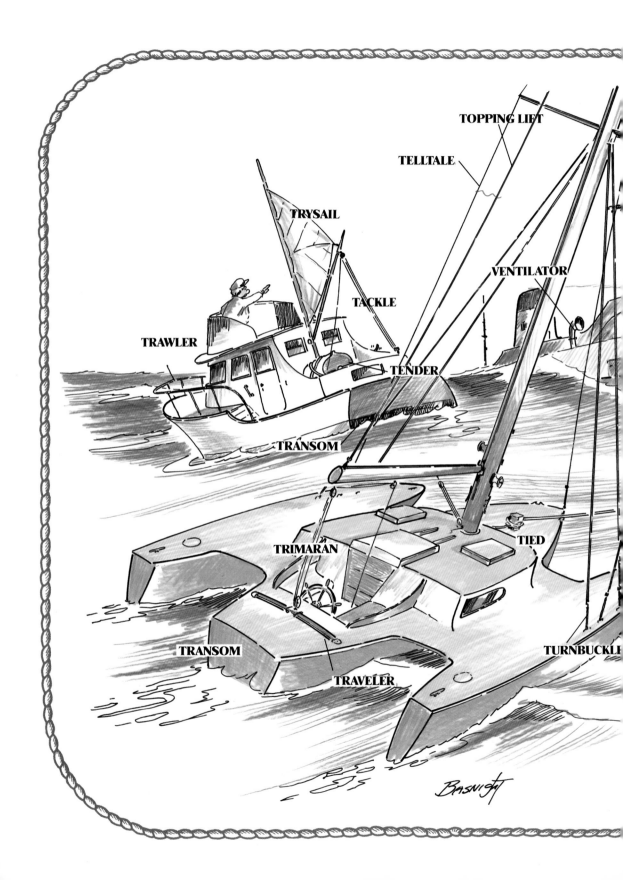

TOPPING LIFT

TELLTALE

TRYSAIL

TACKLE

VENTILATOR

TRAWLER

TENDER

TRANSOM

TIED

TRIMARAN

TRANSOM

TURNBUCKLE

TRAVELER

BASNIGHT

The TELLTALES are flying, and so were Sue and Joe when they won First Place and got the TROPHY! Nearby, Cap'n Bob and Matey help the U.S. COAST GUARD stand by, just in case the TUG needs help.

Later, when they get back to the dock, and the boat ride is over, there will be lots of things to do before leaving. When you go boating, ask the Captain how you can help.

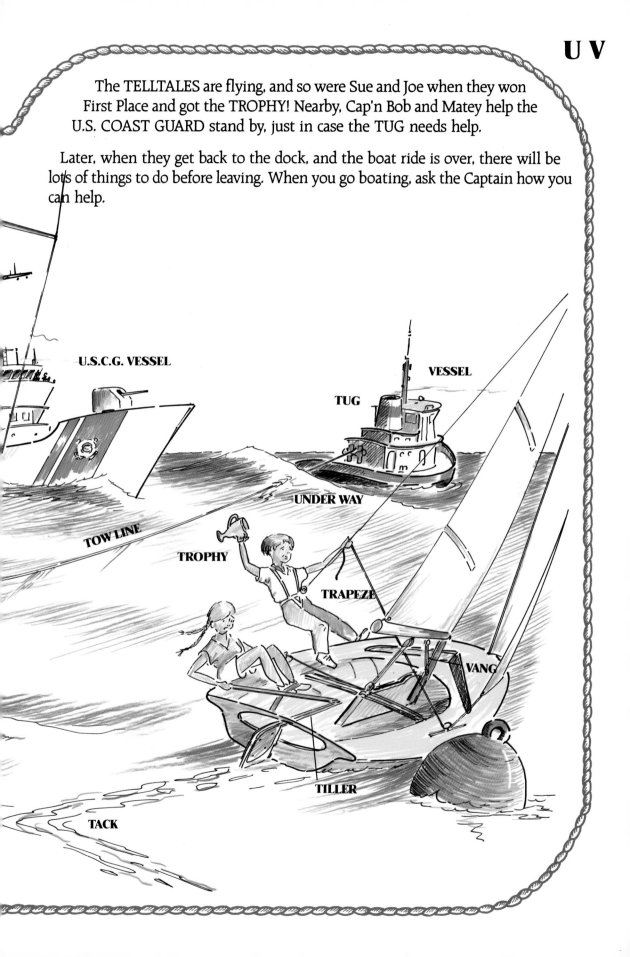

U.S.C.G. VESSEL

VESSEL

TUG

UNDER WAY

TOW LINE

TROPHY

TRAPEZE

VANG

TILLER

TACK

W

Matey climbs over the rocks sniffing for just the right place to dig, while Joe studies the chart near the WRECKAGE. Meanwhile Cap'n Bob waits for the sun to get high in the sky, so he can check his position. They better dig fast! It looks like bad WEATHER coming, and the other boats are leaving now.

If you like boating and like to learn,
Cap'n Bob will invite you back!

YARD

YACHT CLUB

YACHT

WHARF

ZENITH

YACHT

YAWL

ZIPPER

DANGER ZONE

ZONE:
DANGER, RESTRICTED

ZIGZAG

GLOSSARY OF BOATING TERMS

A

Adrift — Floating and free to drift with the wind or current.

Aft — Toward the stern (back end) of a boat.

Aground — Touching bottom, stuck, or stranded.

Aircraft carrier — A large navy warship with a large flat deck, used for airplanes.

Aloft — Up in the rigging above the deck.

Anchor — A heavy metal thing that keeps boats from drifting.

Anchor Chain — A chain connected to an anchor.

Anchor Light — Used to show the location of an anchored boat.

Antenna — A skinny rod or wire, connected to a radio and used to receive or send radio signals.

Apparent Wind Indicator — An arrow that points to the direction the wind seems to be coming from.

Astern — Behind the stern (rear) of a boat.

Awning — A canvas roof or sunshade.

B

Ballast — Weight added to a boat to keep it from turning over.

Barnacles — Small shellfish that stick to things underwater.

Bass Boat — A fast boat made for fishing on fresh water.

Battery — A heavy box or case that holds electricity.

Beach — The sandy shore of an ocean, lake, river or sea.

Beacon — A signal used to help guide boats and airplanes.

Bimini — A sunshade that is attached to the boat.

Bitter End — The end of a line (rope).

Block — A pulley for line (rope) to pass through.

Boarding Ladder — A boat ladder used for climbing aboard.

Boat — A small vessel that is moved by oars, sails or engine.

Boathook — A long pole with a hook used to reach lines (ropes).

Boathouse — A building to keep boats in.

Boatyard — A place that fixes boats.

Boom — A pole that holds out the foot (bottom) of a sail.

Block

Boot Top — A painted line around the water edge of a boat.

Bow — The forward (front) part of a boat.

Bowline — A loop that will not slip and is easy to untie.

Bowspirit — A spar (pole) that sticks out from the bow of a boat.

Bulkhead — A wall. Boats also can have bulkheads.

Buoy — A floating marker.

Burgee — A small flag used by some clubs, or for signals.

C

Cabin — A closed-in room below the decks.

Canal — A man-made waterway.

Canal Barge — A flat-bottomed boat used to carry things.

Can Buoy — A buoy with the shape of a can.

Canoe — A long boat, pointed at both ends and easy to paddle.

Canvas — Sails and cloth covers on a boat.

Captain — The person who gives orders on a boat. The boss.

Cargo — The things for sale carried on a boat.

Cargo Boom — A pole used to help load and unload cargo.

Cargo Hatch — An opening in a boat where cargo is loaded.

Cargo Net — A large net used for lifting cargo.

Chain — Strong metal links connected together.

Chainplate — A metal strap that fastens stays to the hull.

Channel Marker — Used to mark the safe edges of a channel.

Cleat — Has two horns to tie lines (ropes) to.

Clew — The bottom aft (rear) corner of a sail.

Clove Hitch — Two loops of line (rope) with one tucked under.

Cockpit — A protected well in the deck.

Coil — Used to gather a line (rope) in circles for storing.

Compass — Helps show the direction, and always points north.

Cove — A small safe inlet or bay.

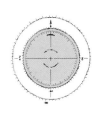

Compass

Creek — A small stream of water.
Crew — Everyone aboard that helps. The captain is their leader.
Cringle — A large eyelet in the edge of a sail.

D

Daggerboard — A centerboard that is moved vertically.
Danforth Anchor — A special lightweight anchor.
Davits — Are used to raise and lower small boats.
Deadeye — A block with three holes used to tighten rigging.
Deck — The top side of a boat.
Deck Pipe — A deck fitting for line or chain to go through.
Dinghy — A small boat usually from a bigger boat.
Dive Flag — A signal used by divers to warn boats to stay away.
Diver — A person that goes down underwater.
Dock — (1) A platform used by boats or ships; (2) the act of bringing a boat into a berth.
Dock Lines — The lines used to tie a boat to a dock.
Double Block — A block with two pulleys to pass lines through.
Downhaul — Any line used to pull down.
Draft Marks — Lines that show how deep a ship is under water.
Drifting — Floating free and moving with the wind or current.

E

East — The general direction of sunrise.
Eddy — A small whirlpool.
Engine — A mechanical device used to put a boat in motion.
Ensign — The national flag used on boats.
Eyebolt — A bolt with an eye on one end.
Eyeplate — A metal plate used to fasten or tie things to.

F

Fairlead — An eye that is used to guide a line.
Fender — A rubber or plastic cushion used to protect boats.
Fenderboard — A cushioned board used to protect boats.
Ferry — A boat used to transport people or cars over water.
Fid — A pointed tool used for opening strands of rope.
Figure Eight Knot — Sometimes used at the end of a line.
Finish — (1) The final coat on a surface; (2) the end of a race.
Fire Extinguisher — Used to put out fires.
Fishing Pole — A pole with a hook and line used to catch fish.
Flag — A colored rectangular cloth with a special meaning.
Flare Gun — A gun used to launch flares when in distress.

Flare — A distress signal which ignites or makes smoke.
Flashing Light — A blinking light used to help find the way.
Floorboards — The flooring in a boat that can be removed.
Flotsam — Floating wreckage (or cargo) from a boat.
Fluke — The tip of an anchor that digs into the ground.
Foremast — The mast nearest the bow (front).

Freighter

Foresail — The sail nearest the bow.
Forestay — The stay from the top of the mast to the bow.
Forward — Toward the bow (toward the front) of a boat.
Framing — The inside framework of a ship or boat.
Freeboard — The height from the waterline to the deck.
Freighter — A ship used to haul freight (cargo).
Furl — To roll or fold a sail and tie it securely.

G

Gaff — A spar used fore and aft across the top of a sail.
Gaff Rig — A four-sided mainsail held by a gaff.
Galley — The kitchen on a boat.
Gas Can — A special can for gasoline.
Genoa Jib — A very large head sail; also called a "gennie."
Gimbals — Can move to keep things level when the boat rocks.
Gooseneck — A hinge to connect a boom to a mast.
Grabrail — Any rail used to hang on to.
Gudgeon — A socket used to connect a rudder to the hull.
Gunwale (Gunnel) — The top of the boat's sides. The rail.
Gust — A sudden rush of wind.

Gimbals

H

Half Hitch — Loops around an object then back around itself.
Halyard — A line used to raise or lower a sail.
Hand Rail — A wooden or metal rail to hold onto.
Hatch — An opening or cover on deck leading below.
Head — The bathroom (toilet) on a boat.
Heeling — Leaning or tipping to one side.
Helm — A tiller or wheel used to steer a boat.
Hobiecat — A type of sailboat with two hulls. A catamaran.
Horizon — Where the earth (or sea) and sky seem to meet.

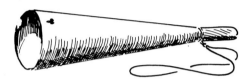

Horn

Horn — To make special sound signals to bridges and boats.
Hose — A flexible tube used for liquids.
Hose Clamp — A metal clamp used to fasten a hose on tightly.
Houseboat — A boat like a house that can be lived on.

I

Inboard Engine — A built-in engine on a boat.
Inflatable — An air inflated boat.
Island — A body of land surrounded by water.

J

J-boat — A special kind (class) of sailboat.
Jetty — A structure built into the water to stop wash (damage) caused by waves or current.
Jib — A triangle sail used on the headstay.
Jib Sheet — A line used to pull in or let out the jib.
Jury Rig — A make-do rig for temporary use.

K

Kayak — An Eskimo canoe that fits snugly around the person paddling.
Keel — The underwater backbone on the bottom of a boat.
Ketch — A sailboat with two masts with the big mast up front.
Knot — A tie point.

L

Ladder — A boat ladder, used to climb aboard.
Lateen Rig — One of the oldest sailboat designs, and still used.

Latitude — Imaginary lines that go around the world (east and west) above and below the equator.

Lazy Jacks — Lines that catch and hold the sails when they come down.

Leak — Any hole or crack that lets water in.

Lead Line — A weighted line with markers used to measure depth.

Leech — The aft (rear) edge of a sail.

Leeward — In the direction away from the wind.

Lifeboat — A boat used for rescue at sea.

Life Jacket — Keeps a person floating while in the water.

Life Raft — An inflatable raft used in an emergency at sea.

Lifting Eye — A strong metal loop used for lifting a load.

Lighthouse — A building with a strong light that guides ships.

Life Jacket

Lines — (1) Ropes on a boat; (2) the shape of a boat.

Listing — Leaning or tilting to one side.

Longitude — Imaginary lines that go up and down (north and south) around the world.

Luff — The front edge of a sail towards the bow.

Luffing — If part of a sail is flapping or fluttering.

M

Mainmast — The tallest mast of a sailboat.

Mainsail — A sail raised on the aft (back) side of the mainmast.

Marlinespike — Used to separate strands of a line for splicing.

Mast — A tall spar (pole) that supports sails.

Mast Step — A place for a mast to sit on top of the keel.

Mid-channel Buoy — A buoy that can be passed on either side.

Mizzenmast — The small mast on the back of a boat with two masts.

Mizzen — A sail set on the mizzenmast.

Monohull — A boat with only one hull.

Mooring Ring — A strong ring used to tie up boats.

Mooring Line — A line (rope) used to tie a boat to a mooring.

Motorboat — A boat propelled by an engine.

Multihull — A boat with two or more hulls.

Mushroom Anchor — A heavy anchor with no flukes to dig in.

N

Navigation Aids — Lights, buoys, and markers with special meanings that help boats stay safe, and find their way.

Navigation Chart — A kind of map used on boats.

Navigation Lights — Used to help boats find the way at night.

Navigator — A person who keeps track of where the boat is.

North Star — A star that is always over the north pole.

Nun Buoy — A floating marker pointed at the top.

O

Oarlock — A U-shaped holder that keeps an oar in place.
Oar — A long pole with a blade, used to row or steer a boat.
Ocean — A great body of water between continents.
Ocean Liner — A large passenger cruise ship.
Ocean Racer — A boat built especially for ocean racing.
Offshore — In the ocean, out of the sight of land.
Oil Lamp — A lamp that is fueled by kerosene.
Oilskins — Waterproof clothing, also called foul-weather gear.
"Old Salt" — A person with lots of experience around boats.
One Design — Boats built all alike for racing.
Outboard Motor — A removable engine for boats.
Outhaul — A line used to adjust the foot (bottom) of a sail.
Overboard — Over the side of a boat or ship.

Oil Lamp

P

Padeye — A metal loop used to fasten things to.
Paddle — A short light pole with a blade at one end and a handle at the other. Used to paddle or steer a boat.
Paint — Paint for boats is usually a special kind.
Palm — A leather pad used to push a needle through canvas.
Parallel Rule — Two hinged slats used for navigation.
Pennant — A long tapered flag used for signaling.
Pier — A platform that goes from land out into the water.
Pile — A pole driven into the ground underwater.
Pintle — A pin that fits into a gudgeon to connect the rudder.
Pliers — A hinged tool with jaws for gripping things.
Planking — The fitted boards on the outside of a boat hull.
Plow Anchor — Has a plow shape that digs into the bottom.
Plug — (1) The put-in end of a power cord; (2) an artificial bait used to catch fish. A lure.
Pole — Any kind of long rod, or spar.
Porgy — A kind of fish.
Port — (1) The left side of a boat when you face forward; (2) a small round window; (3) a harbor where boats usually go.
Porthole — A small round window. A port.
Power Cord — A flexible cord used to plug in for electricity.

Propeller — Has blades and is spun to move boats and planes.

Pulley — A grooved wheel, for line, wire or rope. It changes the direction of the rope.

Pulpit — A strong guardrail around the bow or stern.

Pump — A device used to remove water or other liquids.

Pushpit — A strong guardrail around the stern of a boat.

Propeller

Q

Q-flag — A yellow flag used when entering a foreign country.

Quarter — Either side of a boat's stern.

Quick Action — Thinking fast and doing the right thing.

R

Racer — A boat fast enough for racing.

Radar — Uses radio waves to "see" and help find the way.

Rafting Up — To tie two or more boats beside each other.

Ramp — A roadway into the water for launching or loading boats.

Ratlines — A rope ladder.

Reef Points — Used to tie a sail down to make it smaller.

Rigging — Wires, lines, and gear used to lift and adjust sails.

Ring Buoy — A float that can be thrown to someone in the water.

Roller Furling — A way to stow a sail by rolling it up.

Roller-furling Jib — A jib which is stowed by rolling it up.

Rowboat — A small boat made for rowing.

Rudder — An underwater panel that is turned to steer a boat.

Running Lights — Shows other boats the way a boat is going.

S

Sail Cover — A cover to protect sails from dirt and sunlight.

Sails — Cloth panels used to catch the wind and move a boat.

Samson Post — A very strong post fastened to a boat's keel.

Schooner — Has two or more masts; the forward mast is shortest.

Shackle — A U-shaped metal fitting with a pin across the "U."

Sheer — The curve of the deck on a boat.

Sheet — A line used to trim a sail in or out.

Ship — A vessel large enough to carry another boat.

Shoal — Shallow water that is unsafe.

Shroud — A side stay (wire) that helps hold up the mast.

Signal Flags — Flags used to send signals.

Skipper — The Captain; the person in charge.

Schooner

Sloop — A sailboat with only one mast and only one jib.
Spinnaker — A large ballooning sail. Usually has bright colors.
Spreaders — The struts that help support the mast.
Square Knot — A double knot. Also called a reef knot.
Stanchions — The metal posts that support the lifelines.
Starboard — The right side of a boat when you face forward.
Stay — A wire used to help support the mast.
Stem — The forward (front) edge of the bow.
Stern — The aft (rear) part of the boat.
Stringer — Parts of a boat frame that run fore and aft.

Sloop

T

Tack — (1) Sailing with the wind coming over one side; (2) a turn so the wind crosses over the bow to the other side; (3) the forward lower corner of a sail.
Tackle — Ropes and pulleys used to increase power for pulling.
Telltale — Yarn or ribbon used to show wind direction.
Tender — A small boat used by a larger boat.
Tide — The rise and fall of sea water height.
Tied — When fastened or secured with a line.
Tiller — An arm connected to a boat's rudder for steering.
Topping Lift — Line or wire used to hold up the boom.
Tow Line — A strong line used for towing.
Transom — The stern (rear) surface of a boat.
Trapeze — To use your weight to reduce heeling and go faster.
Traveler — A track and car used to adjust the mainsail.
Trawler — A boat used for pleasure or for fishing with a net.
Trimaran — A boat with three hulls. Also called a multihull.
Trophy — A prize award.
Trysail — A small 3-sided sail used to help steady a boat.
Tug — A workboat used for pushing or towing.
Turnbuckle — Has threaded ends and is used to tighten stays.

Turnbuckle

U

Under Way — Moving in a boat.

Upwind — Toward the direction the wind is blowing from.
U.S.C.G. Vessel — A United States Coast Guard vessel.

V

Vang — Is used to pull down on the boom.
Ventilator (Vent) — Used to get fresh air below decks.
Vessel—Any boat or ship.
Visible Horizon — The line where the sky meets the water.

W

Wake — The churning water and waves left behind a moving boat.
Wash — The effect of wave action on a beach.
Waterline — The water level on a boat's hull.
Wave — A swell moving across the water.
Weather — General conditions, but usually means bad weather.
Weigh Anchor — To raise the anchor.
Wharf — A place to bring ships alongside.
Whisker Pole — A pole or spar used to hold out the jib.
Winch — A drum turned by a handle, used to pull lines.
Winch Handle — A handle used to turn a winch.
Windsurfer — A type of surfboard driven by wind.
Windvane — An arrow that points towards the wind.
Wing and Wing — Sailing with the sails out on opposite sides.
Wishbone Rig — A sailboat with a boom shaped like a wishbone.
Wreckage — The remains of a shipwreck.
Wrinkle — A crease or pucker in sails or cloth.

X

X-Marks-the-Spot — A certain location for something.

Y

Yacht — A pleasure boat.
Yacht Club — A private boat club for members and guests.
Yard — A spar (pole) that supports a square sail.
Yawl — A two-masted boat with the aft mast shortest and aft of the rudder post.

Yawl

Z

Zenith — Straight overhead. The highest place in the sky.
Zephyr — A gentle breeze.
Zigzag — A series of short turns, first one way, then the other.
Zipper — A sliding device used to join two edges of fabric.
Zone (Danger, Restricted) — Areas that require special caution.

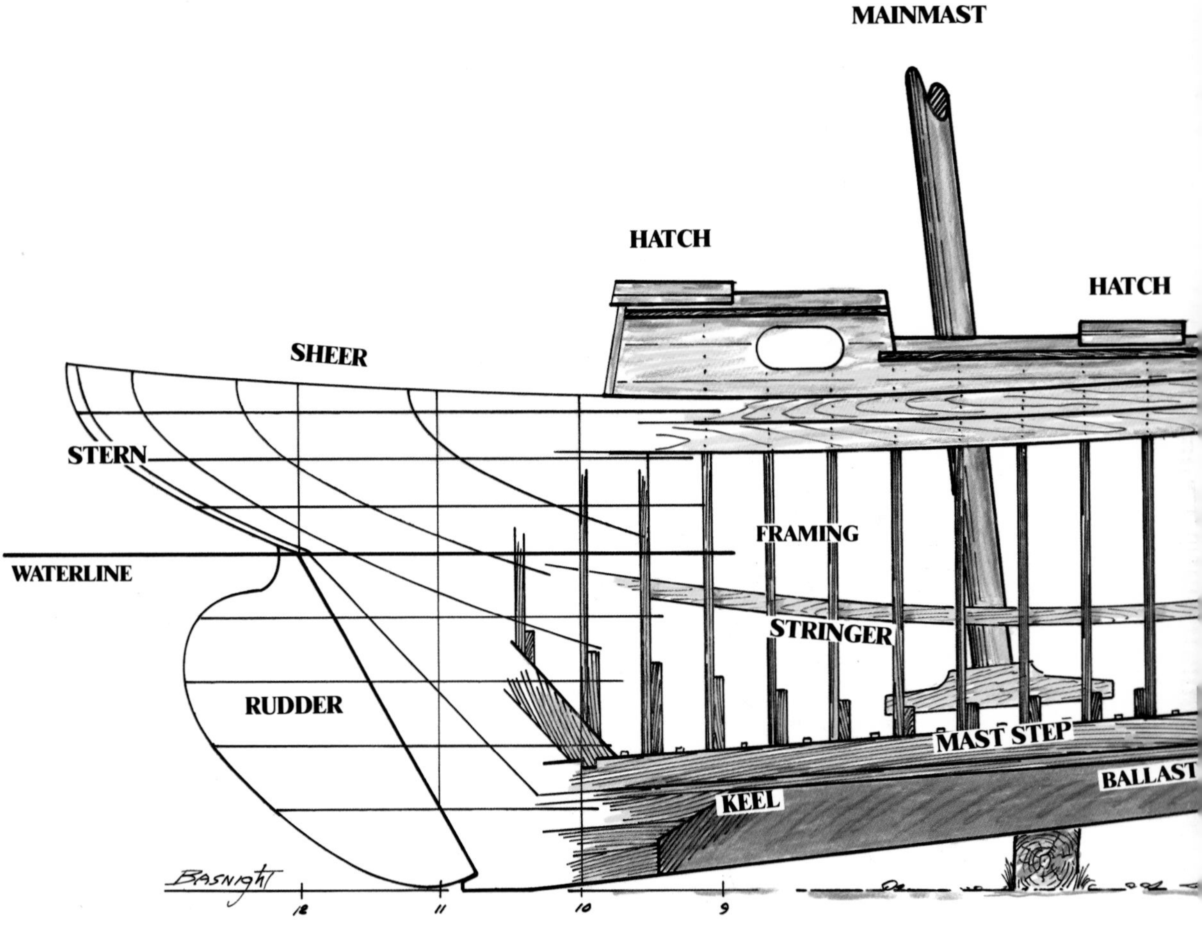

MAINMAST

HATCH

HATCH

SHEER

STERN

FRAMING

WATERLINE

STRINGER

RUDDER

MAST STEP

KEEL

BALLAST

BASNIGHT

12

11

10

9

LINES

FRAMING